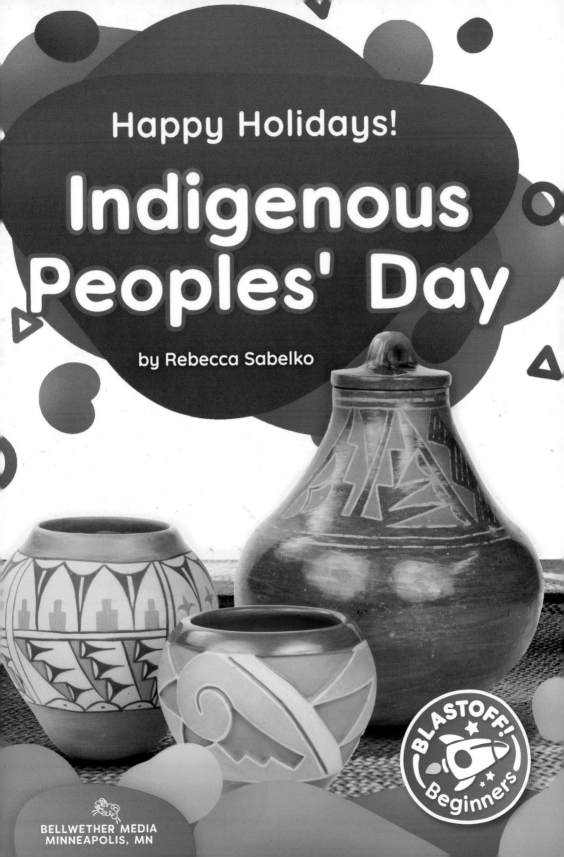

Happy Holidays!

Indigenous Peoples' Day

by Rebecca Sabelko

BELLWETHER MEDIA
MINNEAPOLIS, MN

BLASTOFF!
Beginners

Blastoff! Beginners are developed by literacy experts and educators to meet the needs of early readers. These engaging informational texts support young children as they begin reading about their world. Through simple language and high frequency words paired with crisp, colorful photos, Blastoff! Beginners launch young readers into the universe of independent reading.

Blastoff! Universe

Reading Level — Grade K — Blastoff! Beginners

Grades 1-3 — Blastoff! Readers

Grade 4 — Blastoff! Discovery

Sight Words in This Book 🔍

a	for	is	the	way
about	go	it	their	we
at	have	look	they	
come	help	of	this	
day	in	people	to	

This edition first published in 2023 by Bellwether Media, Inc.

No part of this publication may be reproduced in whole or in part without written permission of the publisher. For information regarding permission, write to Bellwether Media, Inc., Attention: Permissions Department, 6012 Blue Circle Drive, Minnetonka, MN 55343.

Library of Congress Cataloging-in-Publication Data

LC record for Indigenous Peoples' Day available at: https://lccn.loc.gov/2022009276

Text copyright © 2023 by Bellwether Media, Inc. BLASTOFF! BEGINNERS and associated logos are trademarks and/or registered trademarks of Bellwether Media, Inc.

Editor: Christina Leaf   Designer: Laura Sowers

Printed in the United States of America, North Mankato, MN.

Table of Contents

It Is Indigenous Peoples' Day!

We have a lot
to learn.
It is Indigenous
Peoples' Day!

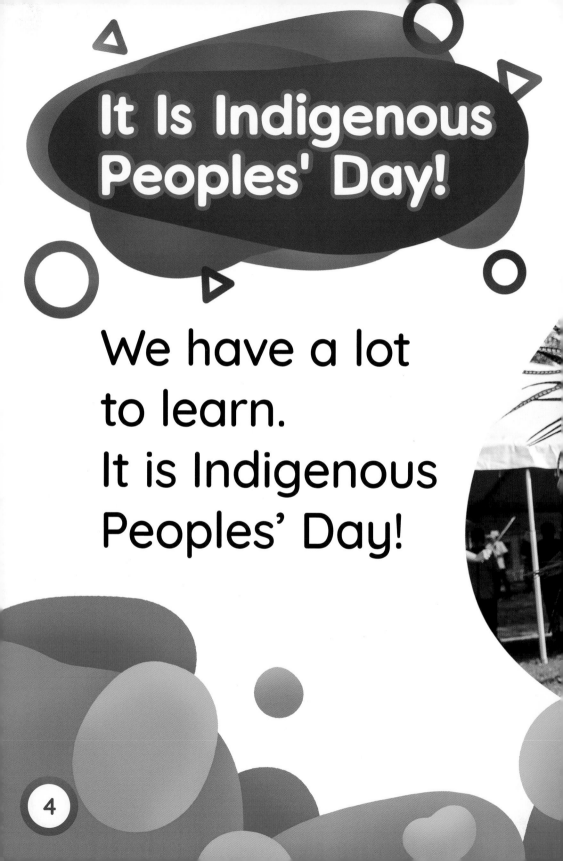

4

A Day to Honor

This day
is in October.
It is the
second Monday.

It honors **Native** people. People learn about their ways of life.

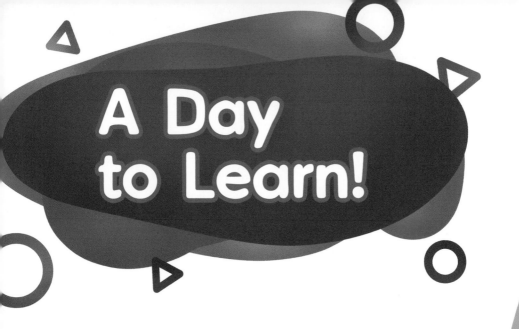

A Day to Learn!

People learn about the past. They read books.

books

People look
at art.

basket

necklace

vases

13

They go
to **events.**
They listen
to music.

14

People
plant seeds.
They help
the land.

People **march**.
They fight for
Native **rights**.

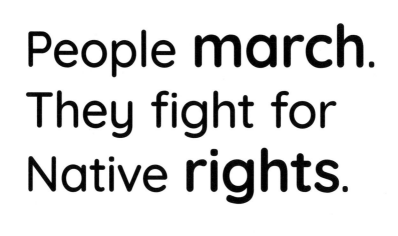

19

Let us remember the past.
Let us work for better days to come!

Indigenous Peoples' Day Facts

Celebrating Indigenous Peoples' Day

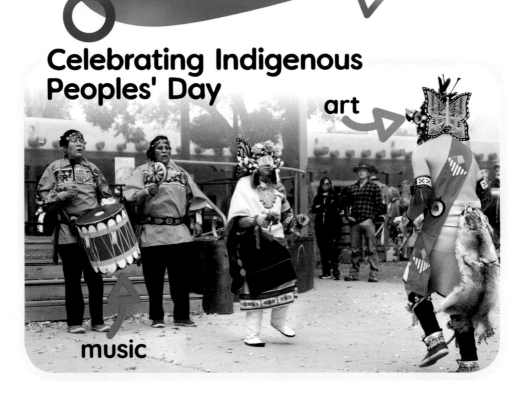

art

music

Indigenous Peoples' Day Activities

go to
events

plant
seeds

march for
rights

Glossary

events

planned
gatherings

march

to walk with others
for change

Native

having began in
the area

rights

freedoms

To Learn More

ON THE WEB

FACTSURFER

Factsurfer.com gives you a safe, fun way to find more information.

1. Go to www.factsurfer.com.

2. Enter "Indigenous Peoples' Day" into the search box and click Q.

3. Select your book cover to see a list of related content.

Index